THE LOST WORLD

John Townsend

Published in association with The Basic Skills Agency

Hodder & Stoughton

A MEMBER OF THE HODDER HEADLINE GROUP

Acknowledgements
Cover: Barry Downard

Photos: p. iv © Chris Butler/Science Photo Library; p. 5 © Bill Varie/CORBIS; p. 11 © BFI Stills; p. 16 © Jim Zuckerman/CORBIS; p. 23 © D. Van Ravenswaay/Science Photo Library; p. 27 © SIPA PRESS/REX FEATURES

Every effort has been made to trace copyright holders of material reproduced in this book. Any rights not acknowledged will be acknowledged in subsequent printings if notice is given to the publisher.

Orders; please contact Bookpoint Ltd, 130 Milton Park, Abingdon, Oxon OX14 4SB. Telephone (44) 01235 827720, Fax: (44) 01235 400454. Lines are open from 9.00–6.00, Monday to Saturday, with a 24 hour message answering service. You can also order through our website www.hodderheadline.co.uk

British Library Cataloguing in Publication Data
A catalogue record for this title is available from the British Library

ISBN 0 340 87145 2

First published 2003
Impression number   10 9 8 7 6 5 4 3 2 1
Year   2007 2006 2005 2004 2003

Typeset by SX Composing DTP, Rayleigh, Essex.
Printed in Great Britain for Hodder & Stoughton Educational, a division of Hodder Headline, 338 Euston Road, London NW1 3BH by Bath Press Ltd, Bath.

Contents

Allosaurus, a large flesh-eating dinosaur.

1 Gone

We live in a new world.
The old has been lost.
Forever.
Or has it?

The Earth hasn't always been as it is now.
It goes back a very long way.
Humans have only been here a short time.
Our planet is full of secrets from the past.

People who dig up the past find new clues each day.
Clues to a lost world.
They tell us about our amazing planet.
We think we know how old the Earth is.
Give or take a few million years.

Think of Earth as an old house.

Lots of lodgers have come and gone down the years.

All very different. They've all left their mark.

Some still lie buried in the garden!

Think of the house as 200 years old.

Today new owners move in.

Only just.

They've been here for a minute or so.

One minute out of 200 years.

That's a bit like how it is with us.

Humans have lived on the Earth for no time at all.

Just a tiny part of a long history.

Just a few moments.

That's all.

And we've hardly had time to unpack!

That's how amazing our world is.

We are only just finding out about its huge past.

We can only guess about
some of the creatures that once lived here.

They've gone for ever.

Perhaps.

Their world has been lost.

Only now can we dig it up and try to find out . . .

2 Monsters

For years no one knew.
Not a clue.
Who could guess huge beasts once ruled the Earth?
Their bones lay in mud for millions of years.

They were dug up bit by bit.
Lots of odd remains.
It took a long time to make sense of them.

Bones began to fit.
Like a huge jigsaw.
People didn't know what it all meant.
Not till 200 years ago.
It took years to work it all out.
We're still finding out.

A dinosaur skeleton at the Natural History Museum, London.

Some bones were massive.
They made huge skeletons.
Monsters.
People were amazed.

But that's not all.
They were shocked.
What if these beasts still lived?
What if some were still out there?
Alive and on the prowl!

It was the start of a new age.
An age of monster stories like never before.
Ideas grew.
Books were soon in the shops.
What if the lost world came back?
It was too scary to think about . . .

3 Stories

A writer had an idea.
Just as more bones were dug up.
He got to work.

His books were already doing well.
They were about a man with a famous pipe and hat.
He could solve any crime.
The stories were of Sherlock Holmes.
It was a name the world knew.
The writer was Arthur Conan Doyle.

But now he wrote a new story.
The title was simple.
It didn't give many clues.
Yet it was soon a real hit.

It was *The Lost World*.
He began a new craze.

The book wasn't any old story.

It was more than a tale of adventure.

It set the way for more.

It came out in 1912.

Many read it.

It made people think.

And panic!

The Lost World was the first of its kind.

The first story about dinosaurs.

Live ones.

It told of a man who set off on a hunt to the jungle.

He went to find a hidden valley.

He'd heard its secret.

It was locked in the past.

A lost world with huge beasts from another age.

The man was Professor Challenger.

He had to find the truth.

So he set off to explore.

He found more than he wanted.

He met living monsters.

Face to face.

The story made people think.

What if such beasts are still out there?

What if one walked into a city?

One did in *The Lost World*.

A monster was on the loose.

Just right for a good horror story.

Arthur Conan Doyle wrote more books.

People loved them.

The subject was scary.

It could happen.

Maybe!

Others wrote new stories.

The idea of a monster coming back took a hold.

Comic books came next.

With scary pictures.

People loved to read them.

Perhaps there really were lost worlds out there.

In time, more and more bones were dug up.
More beasts.
We found new facts.
Hundreds of weird animals once walked the planet.
With every new find came more stories.
More books.

In 1990 Michael Crichton wrote one more.
It was about a theme park full of extinct beasts.
Alive.
Things began to go wrong . . .
The book was a big success.
It was *Jurassic Park*.

Michael Crichton wrote a new book
about dinosaurs.
How they came back to roam the earth.
And the book's name?
You'll never guess.
Just 83 years after the first one.
It was *The Lost World*.

Once more people read of the scary beasts.
Many rushed to see the film . . .

The Lost World.

4 Films

Monsters make good film stars.
People rush to see them at the cinema.
It was the same years ago.
In the early days of film.

The first *Lost World* film came out in 1925.
That was 13 years after the first book.
It was the first time a dinosaur was seen on film.
(Or a rubber one!)
It was a silent film.
It was in black and white.
Even so, it was clever for its day.

Maybe the film now looks 'cheesy'.
We've got used to all the latest hi-tech effects.
But models did the job well.
So did camera tricks.
People in 1925 got a peep into a past world.
A lost one.
But now it was coming back . . . with a bite!

There were new ways to make films.

New tricks. New ideas.

Dinosaurs began to look more real.

The sound got better too.

More films came along.

Each time the effects got more daring.

Then they came on radio and TV.

Lots of them.

They all told the story of a man

who went to find a lost world.

Each time he met a monster.

Face to face.

Or face to teeth.

Each time it looked more real.

The last TV series cost £10 million.

The effects are great.

It's just as if the beasts are real.

They move so life-like. Scary!

Now we're hooked.

CDs, DVDs and games are full of 'lost beasts'.

Books and films keep selling.

We still read about 'The Lost World'.

It's been a hit for over 90 years.

But why?

Why do we care about extinct beasts?

Does it matter what they were really like?

It seems we just need to know.

5 Dino Fever

Today we're mad about dinosaurs.
They're big news.
We see them on TV.
We buy the books.
We get the CDs.
We're still finding out what they were like.

Big!

The BBC showed them looking very real.
Walking With Beasts used clever tricks.

Brachiosaurus, the gentle giant.

Fifty years ago we knew far less.
Fossils tell us new facts all the time.
Each bit fits into the story.
Like a big jigsaw.
It tells us of another world.
Right here.
On our doorstep.

The earth was full of lush plants.
It was warm and wet.
Just right.
Dinosaurs lived all over the world.
Lots of them.
Many sorts.
They were all shapes and sizes.
Some were as small as a cat.
Others were as big as a bus.
Or much bigger . . .

One was huge.
It was a gentle giant.
Its name is big too!
It was a *brachiosaurus*.
It was about 60 metres long.
And it was heavy.
About 150 tonnes.
That's big!
All day it ate leaves.
By the tree load.

Other beasts were far more scary.
They ate meat.
Lots of it.
They hunted in packs.
It's just as well we weren't around.
They'd eat people like sweets!

If you met an *allosaurus* you wouldn't last long.
Its teeth would rip you apart.
Its jaws could open very wide.
It was very strong.
It would grip, rip and snip all in one go!

Get out of the Way of BIG AL!

T.rex was bad news.
It could kill most things.
It ate meat all the time.
It was 12 metres long.
It was as tall as a house.
It lived till 65 million years ago.
If it ever came back . . . run!
It could eat a man in one go.
You'd be gone in one gulp!

Then there were beasts in the sky.
Flying lizards.
Great birds that could carry you off.
Claws and teeth just above you.
Lots of huge beaks.

The Lost World must have been a scary place.
It seems the earth was like this for millions of years.
Will it ever return?
Some say it might.
Who can be sure?

6 Did You Know?

Many people study fossils.
They tell us all sorts of facts.
At times we can only guess.
We think we know a lot.
Even so, it's just the 'bare bones'.
There's still a lot to find out.

Here are ten facts from the 'dino files':

- Dinosaurs died out about 65 million years ago.
- They all laid eggs.
- The first eggs were found in 1922.
  Some were 40 cm long.
- The name dinosaur means 'big lizard'.
  It was first used about 160 years ago.
- They lived in the Mesozoic Age.
  That's 245 to 65 million years ago.
  A long time!
- So far we know 300 types of dinosaur.
  There may have been 1500.
  So we may only know 20%
  of what there is to know!
- Fossil comes from the Latin for 'dug up'.
- A *t.rex* may have lived for 100 years or more.
- The heart of the biggest dinosaur was heavy.
  About a tonne!
- If dinosaurs hadn't died out
  we might not be here today!

To see more you can look at a few web sites.

Beware – some beasts may come to life!

You may hear some too.

You can try to find the lost world.

If you dare . . .

- www.bbc.co.uk/dinosaurs/
- www.search4dinosaurs.com/a2d.htm
- www.prehistorics.com/contents.htm%20T-REX.htm
- dsc.discovery.com/guides/dinosaur/dinosaur.html

You can find more about 'walking with beasts' on TV and in films.

To see more about the story of 'The Lost World', look at:

- www.bbc.co.uk/drama/lostworld/index.shtml

- silentmoviemonsters.tripod.com/TheLostWorld/index.html

Happy surfing!

A *t.rex* runs from a meteor.

7 Where Did They Go?

So the earth was full of huge beasts.
They ruled for millions of years.
But all of a sudden they went.
Gone. Lost.
Why?

It's a big mystery.
What made them die out?
65 million years ago the world changed.
No one knows why. Not for sure.

Perhaps the end came from above.
Did a vast meteor hit the earth?
Some say it was like a huge atom bomb.
It sent a shock over all the earth.
Red-hot rocks fell from the sky.
The sea swept over the land.
Dust and smoke hid the sun.
All went dark and cold.
Life was wiped out.

Or maybe the 'bomb' was deep inside the earth.
Did a huge volcano blow up?
Did it set off lots of others?
If so, the shocks could kill.
Ash and gas would fill the sky.
The sea would boil.
Lava would kill all the trees.
Then came the ice age.
The earth froze.
Nothing lived.

Or did the beasts just get ill?
Did a killer bug go wild?
Maybe germs hit all life on earth.
Perhaps a virus got rid of the lot.

So it all came to an end.
The huge beasts died.
They fell into mud.
Their bones lay locked in rock for millions of years.

Until now.
Now we dig them up.
At last they are back in the light.
As they begin to live again!

8 What if . . .

Can the lost world ever come back?
Will dinosaurs really live again?
Some say there are still a few left.
Just like in *The Lost World*.
Now and again people say they see odd things.
In remote jungles.
Huge beasts. Prints in the mud. Roars.
You never know!

After the dinosaurs died out,
other life took a hold.
Big mammals didn't mind the cold.
They lived in the Ice Age.
But even they died out in time.
Just a few thousand years ago.
Maybe humans killed them all.

Mammals like
• Woolly mammoths
• Woolly rhinos
• Sabre tooth cats.

A wooly mammoth.

Bodies are found each year.
In ice or in tar pits.
Some are whole. Almost perfect.
They are taken to labs.
Their cells can be used.
The DNA of a woolly mammoth is already in use.

One day they hope to make new life.
From DNA in a test tube.
They may be able to clone a baby mammoth.
If it works, where will it all end?
Will they do the same to other extinct beasts?

It may not be as crazy as it seems.
You never know what you may see in the pet shop!

They say it's 'The Lost World'.
Gone for good.
Never to return.
But just think . . .

Things that are lost can be found.
Now and again.
So keep looking!
They may be back . . .